*Cornerstones*

*of*

# SUCCESS

Great Quotations, Inc.

Written by Patrick Caton
Cover Design and typography by Dmitry Feygin

Published by Great Quotations Publishing Co.,
Glendale Heights, IL

Library of Congress Catalog Card Number: 96-078972

ISBN 1-56245-279-7

Printed in Hong Kong 2000

# Dedication:

To Joe, Tim, Brian and Sean,
and Brian Kerry, a. k. a.
"Señor Success"

Success is the maximum utilization of
the ability that you have.
*Zig Ziglar*

Success has always been easy to
measure. It is the distance between
one's origins and one's
final achievement.

*Michael Korda*

I do the very best I know how – the very best I can and I mean to keep on doing so until the end.

*Abraham Lincoln*

Success is having a flair for the thing
that you are doing; knowing that is not
enough, that you have got to have hard
work and a certain sense of purpose.

*Margaret Thatcher*

Whenever a man does the best he can,
then that is all he can do.

*Harry S. Truman*

I want to be all that
I am capable of becoming.
*Katherine Mansfield*

Surely a man has come to himself only when he has found the best that is in him, and has satisfied his heart with the highest achievement he is fit for.

*Woodrow Wilson*

10

How far you go in life depends on
your being tender with the young,
compassionate with the aged,
sympathetic with the striving and
tolerant of the weak and strong.
Because some day you
will have been all of these.

*George Washington Carver*

11

The future belongs to those who
believe in the beauty of their dreams.

*Eleanor Roosevelt*

It's not half as important to burn the
midnight oil as it is to be awake
in the daytime.

*E. W. Elmore*

No one ever attains very eminent success by simply doing what is required of him; it is the amount and excellence of what is over and above the required, that determines the greatness of ultimate distinction.

*Charles Kendall Adams*

14

You may be disappointed if you fail,
but you are doomed if you don't try.

*Beverly Sils*

The price of success is hard work, dedication to the job at hand and the determination that whether we win or lose, we have applied the best of ourselves to the task at hand.

*Vince Lombardi*

16

Effort is a commitment to seeing a task through to the end, not just until you get tired of it.
*Howard Cato*

The heights by great men reached and kept were not attained by sudden flight, but they while their companions slept, were toiling upward in the night.

*Henry Wadsworth Longfellow*

By patience and hard work, we brought order out of chaos, just as will be true of any problem if we stick to it with patience and wisdom and earnest effort.

*Booker T. Washington*

Nothing good comes in life or athletics unless a lot of hard work has preceded the effort. Only temporary success is achieved by taking short cuts.

*Roger Staubach*

20

If hard work is the key to success,
most people would rather
pick the lock.

*Claude McDonald*

It is certain that the greatest poets, orators, statesmen and historians, men of the most brilliant and imposing talents, have labored as hard, if not harder, than day laborers; and that the most obvious reason why they have been superior to other men is that they have taken more pains than other men.

*Orison Swett Marden*

If we do what is necessary, all the
odds are in our favor.

*Henry Kissinger*

23

We are one, our cause is one,
and we must help each other,
if we are to succeed.

*Frederick Douglass*

24

Luck is a dividend of sweat.  The
more you sweat the luckier you get.

*Ray Kroc*

From now on, any definition of a
successful life must include
serving others.

*George Bush*

26

You can't build a reputation on
what you're going to do.
*Henry Ford*

Take time to deliberate, but when the time for action has arrived, stop thinking and go for it.

*Napoleon Bonaparte*

All you need in this life is ignorance
and confidence, and then
success is sure.

*Mark Twain*

29

The important thing is
not to stop questioning.
*Albert Einstein*

30

I dare to do all that may become a
man: who dares do more is none.
*William Shakespeare*

There are two big forces at work,
external and internal.  We have
very little control over such
forces as tornados, earthquakes,
floods, disasters, illness and pain.
What really matters is the
internal force.  How do I respond to
those disasters?  Over that I have
complete control.

*Leo Buscaglia*

32

It takes a person with
a mission to succeed.
*Clarence Thomas*

It takes twenty years to make an
overnight success.

*Eddie Cantor*

34

Success comes to a writer, as a rule,
so gradually, that it is always
something of a shock to him
to look back and realize the heights to
which he has climbed.

*P.G. Wodehouse*

35

The reason a lot of people do not
recognize opportunity is because it
usually goes around looking
like hard work.

*Thomas Alva Edison*

36

Do what you can, with what you have,
where you are.

*Theodore Roosevelt*

The man who works for the gold in the
job rather than the money in the pay
envelope, is the fellow who gets on.

*Joseph French Johnson*

38

The boy who is going to make a great man must not make up his mind not merely to overcome a thousand obstacles, but to win in spite of a thousand repulses and defeats.

*Theodore Roosevelt*

39

There is one plain rule of life. Try thyself unweariedly till thou findest the highest thing thou art capable of doing, faculties and outward circumstances being both duly considered, and then do it.

*John Stuart Mill*

40

To have known the best, and to have
known it for the best, is
success in life.

*John W. MacKay*

I can't imagine a person becoming a success who doesn't give this game of life everything he's got.

*Walter Cronkite*

42

Everybody can be great, because
anybody can serve.
*Martin Luther King, Jr.*

To be successful, the first thing to do
is fall in love with your work.

*Sister Mary Lauretta*

44

There is a brilliant child locked
inside every student.
*Marva Collins*

Success isn't everything, but it makes
a man stand straight.

*Lillian Hellman*

Success is like a liberation or the first phase of a love affair.

*Jeanne Moreau*

No one can possibly achieve any real
and lasting success or get rich in
business by being a conformist.

*J. Paul Getty*

48

Anytime you see someone more
successful than you are, they are
doing something that you aren't.
*Malcolm X*

Success lies solely in the heart of the man. One can not find it in time, place or circumstance.

*Brian Kerry*

50

The first and best victory is to
conquer self.

*Plato*

There's a way to do it better—find it.
*Thomas Edison*

52

A sad soul can kill you quicker, far quicker, than a germ.

*John Steinbeck*

53

Always be smarter than the people
who hire you.
*Lena Horne*

We ought not to look back unless
it is to derive useful lessons
from past errors.
*George Washington*

55

Children's talent to endure stems from
their ignorance of alternatives.
*Maya Angelou*

Even when I went to the playground, I never picked the best players.  I picked the guys with less talent, but who were willing to work hard...and put in the effort, who had the desire to be great.

*Earvin "Magic" Johnson*

Success is a state of mind.  If you
want success, start thinking of
yourself as a success.

*Joyce Brothers*

58

Make the most of yourself, for that is
all there is of you.

*Ralph Waldo Emerson*

You never really lose until
you stop trying.
*Mike Ditka*

The question: "Who ought to be boss?" is like saying "Who ought to be the tenor in the quartet?" Obviously, the man who can sing tenor.

*Henry Ford, Sr.*

61

There is only one success—to be able
to spend your life in your own way.

*Christopher Morley*

As I grow older, I pay less attention to what men say. I just watch what men do.

*Andrew Carnegie*

63

I made a resolve then that I was going
to amount to something if I could.
And no hours, nor amount of labor,
nor amount of money would deter me
from giving the best that there was in
me. And I have done that ever since,
and I win by it. I know.

*Colonel Harland Sanders*

64

A good manager is one who isn't worried about his own career but rather the careers of those who work for him.

*H.S.M. Burns*

Success consists in the climb.

*Elbert Hubbard*

I've never sought success in order to
get fame and money; It's the talent
and the passion that
count in success.

*Ingrid Bergman*

The man who is sure to advance is the one who is too big for his place.

*Wallace D. Wattles*

Don't ever confuse motion with progress.

*Hadley's Law*

Along with success comes a
reputation for wisdom.
*Alexandre Dumas*

Don't bother about genius. Don't worry about being clever. Trust to hard work, perseverance and determination.

*Sir Frederick Treves*

The ability to accept responsibility is
the measure of the man.

*Roy L. Smith*

The top is not forever.  Either you walk down or you are going to be kicked down.

*Janet Collins*

Bravery is the capacity to perform
even when scared half to death.

*Omar Bradley*

74

We are not interested in the
possibilities of defeat.

*Queen Victoria*

People succeed because they believe,
not only that they can and will
succeed, but also that success is
worth the price they pay for it.

*Tom Hopkins*

You gain strength, courage and confidence by every experience in which you really stop to look fear in the face.

*Eleanor Roosevelt*

Parents can only give good advice or put them on the right paths, but the final forming of a person's character lies in their own hands.

*Anne Frank*

Measure not the work until the day's
out and the labor done.

*Elizabeth Barrett Browning*

Success is not the result of
spontaneous combustion.  You must
set yourself on fire.

*Reggie Leach*

80

Life does not require us to make good;
it only asks that we give our best at
each level of experience.

*Harold W. Ruopp*

81

Do what you can, with what you have,
where you are.

*Theodore Roosevelt*

Behind an able man there are
always other able men.
*Chinese Proverb*

83

I've always believed that one woman's success can only help another woman's success.

*Gloria Vanderbilt*

84

I have not failed.  I have
discovered twelve hundred
materials that don't work.
*Thomas Edison*

Your success and happiness
lie in you.
*Helen Keller*

One can present people with opportunities. One cannot make them equal to them.

*Rosamond Lehmann*

Only yourself can heal you,
Only yourself can lead you.

*Sara Teasdale*

88

Integrity is so perishable in the
summer months of success.

*Vanessa Redgrave*

89

I do not try to dance better than anyone else. I only try to dance better than myself.

*Mikhail Baryshnikov*

90

What is success?  It is a toy balloon among children armed with pins.

*Gene Fowler*

91

Success is counted sweetest,
By those who never succeed.

*Emily Dickinson*

Whoever employs you does so for a
selfish motive.  You must be
worth more to him than the
money he pays you.
*David Seabury*

The respect that is only bought by
gold is not worth much.

*Frances Ellen Watkins Harper*

Example is more efficacious
than precept.
*Samuel Johnson*

Leadership is the ability to get
men to do what they don't want
to do and like doing it.

*Harry Truman*

96

The successful person is the one who
went ahead and did the thing
I always intended to do.

*Ruth Smeltzer*

I never wanted to set records.  The
only thing I strived for was perfection.

*Wilt Chamberlain*

The first step toward getting somewhere is to decide that you are not going to stay where you are.

*J. Morgan & E. Webb*

All the great things are simple.

*Winston Churchill*

100

Help thy brother's boat across, and lo!
Thine own has reached the shore.

*Hindu Proverb*

101

Success seems to be connected with action. Successful men keep moving. They make mistakes, but they don't quit.

*Conrad Hilton*

102

You never get ahead of anyone as long
as you try to get even with him.
*Lou Holtz*

103

Failures are like skinned knees—
painful but superficial.

*H. Ross Perot*

104

The great thing in this world is not so much where we are but in what direction we are moving.

*Oliver Wendell Holmes*

105

The greatest mistake a man can make
is to be afraid of making one.
*Elbert Hubbard*

106

Failure is success if we learn from it.
*Malcolm Forbes*

Coming together is a beginning.
Keeping together is progress.
Working together is success.

*Henry Ford, Sr.*

A wise man will make more
opportunities than he finds.

*Francis Bacon*

When you get to the end of your rope,
tie a knot and hang on.

*Franklin Roosevelt*

Greatness is so often a courteous
synonym for great success.

*Guedalla*

111

Man dies when he refuses to stand up
for that which is right.  A man dies
when he refuses to take a stand for
that which is true.

*Martin Luther King, Jr.*

112

If you could get the courage to begin,
you have the courage to succeed.

*David Viscott*

Always do your best.  What you plant
now, you will harvest later.

*Og Mandino*

114

Success is the greatest thing in the world—I'll tell you why. Without it, a man is a failure.

*Clare Kummer*

115

Even if you're on the right track,
you'll get run over if you just sit there.
*Will Rogers*

The best career advice to give the young is, "Find out what you like doing best and get someone to pay you for doing it."

*Katherine Whitehorn*

117

The common idea that success spoils people by making them vain, egotistic and self-complacent is erroneous.  On the contrary, it makes them, for the most part, humble, tolerant and kind. Failure makes people bitter and cruel.

*W. Sommerset Maugham*

118

The world is an oyster, but you don't
crack it open on a mattress.
*Arthur Miller*

The secret of success lies not in doing your own work, but in recognizing the right man to do it.

*Andrew Carnegie*

120

If you can imagine it, you can achieve it.  If you can dream it, you can become it.

*William Arthur Ward*

All our dreams can come true, if we
have the courage to pursue them.

*Walt Disney*

Procrastination is opportunity's natural assassin.

*Victor Kiam*

What I do is prepare myself until I
know I can do what I have to do.

*Joe Namath*

124

The toughest thing about success
is that you've got to keep on
being a success.
*Irving Berlin*

Success is something to enjoy, to flaunt! Otherwise, why work so hard to get it?

*Isobel Lennart*

126

It's never finished.  There's always the
next objective, the next goal.

*Moya Lear*

The penalty of success is to be bored
by people who used to snub you.

*Nancy Astor*

Things turn out best for the people
who make the best of the way
things turn out.

*John Wooden*

It is a mistake to suppose that men succeed through success; they much oftener succeed through failures...Precept, study, advice and example could never have taught them so well as failure has done.

*Samuel Smiles*

130

The object of business is not
to make others comfortable,
but to make them successful.

*Laurel Cutler*

131

# The proof of gold is fire.

*Benjamin Franklin*

Take your life into your own hands,
and what happens?  A terrible thing:
no one to blame.

*Erica Jong*

We will either find a way or make one.

*Hannibal*

Success is the child of audacity.
*Disraeli*

135

It is not the going out of port, but the coming in, that determines the success of the voyage.

*H.W. Beecher*

136

Actually, all I ever wanted to be was
the best in my field.

*Lou Holtz*

You don't pay the price for success.
You enjoy the price for success.
*Zig Ziglar*

138

A man, as a general rule, owes very
little to what he is born with—a man
is what he makes of himself.

*Alexander Graham Bell*

Nothing in the world can take the
place of persistence.

*Calvin Coolidge*

140

What's important is that one
strives to achieve a goal.
*Ronald Reagan*

History knows no resting places
and no plateaus.

*Henry Kissinger*

There's no heavier burden than
a great potential.
*Charles M. Schultz*

He who is not courageous
enough to take risks will
accomplish nothing in life.
*Muhammad Ali*

He who has done his best for his own
time has lived for all times.

*Johann Frederich von Schiller*

To be successful, grow to the
point where one completely
forgets himself; that is, to lose
himself in a great cause.

*Booker T. Washington*

146

I am not judged by the number of times I fail, but by the number of times I succeed; and the number of times I succeed is in direct proportion to the number of times I can fail and keep on trying.

*Tom Hopkins*

Success is the result of perfection,
hard work, learning from failure,
loyalty and persistence.

*Colin Powell*

Keeping a little ahead of business is
one of the secrets of business.

*Charles M. Schwab*

One man has enthusiasm for 30
minutes, another for 30 days, but it is
the man who has it for 30 years who
makes a success of his life.

*Edward B. Butler*

150

The men who succeed best in public life are those who take the risk of standing by their own convictions.

*James A. Garfield*

They say getting thin is the best revenge.  Success is much better.

*Oprah Winfrey*

You can't base your life on other
people's expectations.

*Stevie Wonder*

Help people become more
motivated by guiding them to
the source of their own power.
*Paul G. Thomas*

154

You never work for someone else.
The truth is, someone is paying
you to work for yourself.
*Paul J. Meyer*

I must admit that I personally measure success in terms of the contributions an individual makes to her or his fellow human beings.

*Margaret Mead*

The world is moving so fast these days
that the man who says it can't be done is
generally interrupted by someone doing it.

*Harry Emerson Fosdick*

157

The first and most important step
toward success is the feeling
that we can succeed.

*Nelson Boswell*

Success and failure are not true
opposites and they're not even
in the same class; they're not
even a couch and a chair.
*Lillian Hellman*

159

Success is not achieved by working until
the whistle sounds at the end of the day
but by working even though the whistle
has sounded at the end of the day.

*Roderick Van Murchison*

160

In every case, expect the sun, the moon & the stars. Settle for the sun & the moon.

*Thom Munsen*

161

Life's garden is filled with seeds of success. Failures are simply fertilizer for the soil.

*Monica Kazmier*

162

You don't start climbing a mountain to get to the middle.  Why be content with being average?

*James Hart*

163

Everyone has the potential for success.
Hard work and commitment are the
best ways to actualize this potency.

*Thomas Clary*

I have observed that to succeed
in the world one should appear
like a fool but be wise.

*Montesquieu*

A man is a success if he gets up in
the morning and goes to bed at night
and in between does
what he wants to do.
*Bob Dylan*

Little successes pave the way to
bigger successes.

*Mary Kay Ash*

167

## Other Titles by Great Quotations

301 Ways to Stay Young At Heart
African-American Wisdom
A Lifetime of Love
A Light Heart Lives Long
Angel-grams
As A Cat Thinketh
A Servant's Heart
Astrology for Cats
Astrology for Dogs
A Teacher is Better Than Two Books
A Touch of Friendship
Can We Talk
Celebrating Women
Chicken Soup
Chocoholic Reasonettes
Daddy & Me
Dare to Excel
Erasing My Sanity
Falling in Love
Fantastic Father, Dependable Dad
Golden Years, Golden Words
Graduation Is Just The Beginning
Grandma, I Love You
Happiness is Found Along The Way

High Anxieties
Hooked on Golf
I Didn't Do It
Ignorance is Bliss
I'm Not Over the Hill
Inspirations
Interior Design for Idiots
Let's Talk Decorating
Life's Lessons
Life's Simple Pleasures
Looking for Mr. Right
Midwest Wisdom
Mommy & Me
Mom's Homemade Jams
Mother, I Love You
Motivating Quotes for Motivated People
Mrs. Murphy's Laws
Mrs. Webster's Dictionary
My Daughter, My Special Friend
Only a Sister
Parenting 101
Pink Power
Read the Fine Print

Reflections
Romantic Rhapsody
Size Counts !
Social Disgraces
Sports Prose
Stress or Sanity
The ABC's of Parenting
The Be-Attitudes
The Birthday Astrologer
The Cornerstones of Success
The Rose Mystique
The Secret Language of Men
The Secret Language of Women
The Secrets in Your Face
The Secrets in Your Name
TeenAge of Insanity
Thanks from the Heart
The Lemonade Handbook
The Mother Load
The Other Species
Wedding Wonders
Words From The Coach
Working Woman's World

**Great Quotations Publishing Company**
1967 Quincy Court
Glendale Heights, IL 60139, U.S. A.
Phone: 630-582-2800     Fax: 630-582-2813
http: //www.greatquotations.com